Christmas Flowers

MARK J. WESTON

Flower Arrangements by Jane Weston   **Photography by Roger Tuff**

FOUR SEASONS PUBLICATIONS
The Stables, Monxton, Nr. Andover, Hants, SP11 8AT

GW00993699

Reproduction by Colourcraftsmen Ltd.,
Chelmsford, Essex
Printed in Great Britain by
Tindal Press, Chelmsford, Essex

SBN 9011 31 09 1

CONTENTS

WIRING A LEAF

1. Thin reel wire is stitched through the leaf from behind. The stitch is on either side of the central rib about half-way down the leaf. The wire is then cut from the reel to give two equal wire legs of the desired length.

2. The two wire legs are paralleled and taken down on either side of the central rib to project about 2 to 3 in. below the stem. One leg is then wound around the other leg and the base of the leaf.

3. The leaf is now fully wired and the two wire legs can be used to insert into the arrangement.

A similar technique can be used for any individual leaf whether big or small.

2.

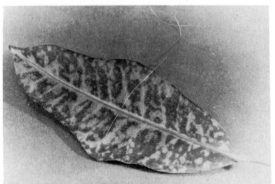

1.

3.

WIRING A FIR CONE

1. A 10 in. by 22° wire is threaded around the cone between the layer of seed husks so that an equal length of wire projects on either side of the cone.

2. The two wire legs are each brought downwards to the stem. One leg is then wound around the other leg and the stem itself.

3. The cone is now fully wired and the two projecting wire legs are parallel and ready for insertion as required.

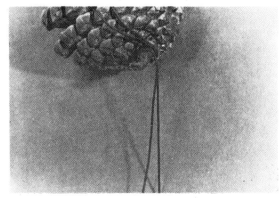

2.

1.

3.

'POLYFILLA'

MAKING A RIBBON ROSE

1. 'Polyfilla' or alabastine is mixed with water to a stiff putty-like consistency. The ingredients for the decoration must be inserted before the mixture sets. 'Polyfilla' usually allows at least 30 minutes for this purpose but alabastine sets much quicker.
If large items are inserted into the 'Polyfilla' they will require support until they are properly held in position by the setting mixture.

2. The first fold of the ribbon is illustrated
3. The second fold. Notice how a square is being formed.
4. The first ribbon square has now been assembled.

3.

1.

2.

4.

5. Continue making further squares from the same continuous length of ribbon until eight squares (approx.) have been assembled one on top of the other. Make sure that a central hole remains throughout the assembly.

6. The ribbon has now been cut from the reel and a two-legged wire is wound around the end. (see page 10 for wiring technique). The two-legged wire is threaded through the top of the central hole and the ribbon is drawn through.

7. The centre of the Rose has now been made and all that remains is for the stem to be covered with gutta-percha tape.

8. The back of the Rose showing taped stem ready to be inserted into an arrangement.

 5.

 7.

 6.

 8.

GREEN AND GOLD ARRANGEMENT

1.

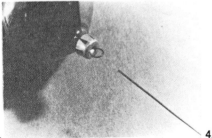

3

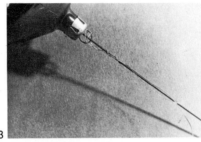

2.

4.

A triangular arrangement consisting of gilded grevillea and populus foliage, green dyed bullrushes, green teazles, wood roses, baubles, loops of ribbon (see page 36) and ribbon roses (see pages 6 and 7).

Wiring a Bauble

1. The 'Oasis' container with block of 'Oasis' rather than a cylinder. This allows a bigger area of 'Oasis' for ingredient insertion.

2. A 12 in. by 22° wire is about to be inserted into the hollow neck of the bauble.

3. The wire having been inserted is bound into position with silver reel wire (5 amp fuse wire could be substituted).

4. A roll of gutta-percha (a latex binding tape) has been used around the neck and down the stem to bind and cover the exposed wires.

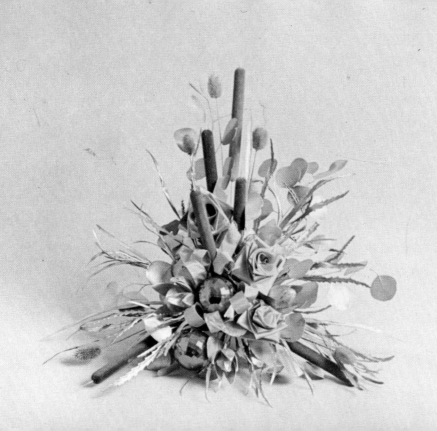

HANGING EVERGREEN BALL

1.

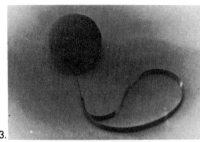

3.

2.

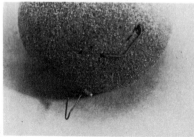

4.

This festive decoration includes the following: blue pine, green and variegated holly, cupressus (see page 14 for wiring), ivy, berries and ribbon loops (see page 36).

1. Shows the 'Oasis' ball, which has been used in the middle, with ribbon handle attached.

Making the Ribbon Handle

2. A 12 in. by 22° wire has been made into a hairpin shape and one leg has been wound twice around the other and the ends of the ribbon loop and then allowed to become the second leg of the hairpin again.

3. Shows the wire being thrust completely through the 'Oasis' ball.

4. Shows the two legs of the wire mount projecting through the bottom of the 'Oasis' ball and being turned back and pushed home to provide a secure fixing.

WINTER BRANCH

A carefully selected bare branch has been silvered and stuck into 'Polyfilla' (see page 6)—which has been heaped onto a piece of cork bark. The 'Polyfilla' base is decorated and screened with fir cones and lichen moss. The tree is hung with baubles.

Wiring Lichen Moss

1. A piece of Reindeer moss, well soaked to eliminate brittleness, has had a 7 in. by 22° hairpinned wire placed at the back of the moss.
2. One leg of the hairpin is wound around the other leg and the bottom of the moss providing a two-legged mount.
3. Shows a close-up of the back of the mounted moss.
4. Showing wired fir cones (see page 5) and lichen moss inserted into 'Polyfilla' (see page 6).

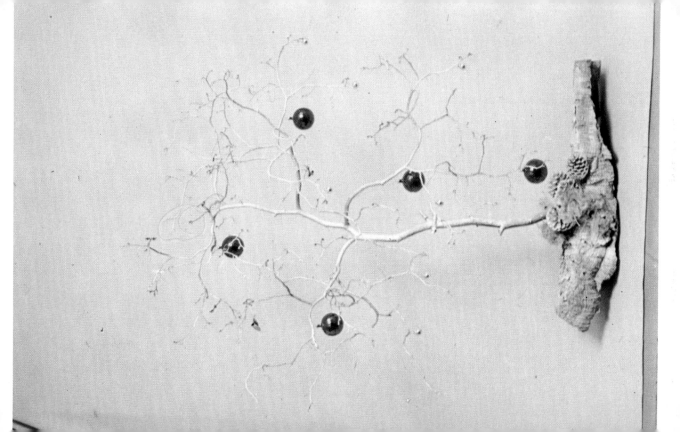

KISSING BOUGH

Mounted pine and holly foliage has been bound onto the special frame using the legs of the mounts for this purpose. A number of ribbons, each with a bauble attached, are fixed to the top of the Bough and a ribbon handle and bow finish off the decoration.

Frame for Kissing Bough

1. Three outer rings from wreath frames are separated to supply the circles for the Bough.

Alternatively rings can be made (of equal diameter) from ordinary wire of reasonable thickness.

The three rings are then assembled as shown and bound at each meeting point with *thin wire*.

Wiring Evergreen Foliage

2. A wire (7 in. by 22°) has been placed at the back of the sprig of foliage.
3. The wire is made into a hairpin and one leg is wound around the other and the base of the foliage sprig.

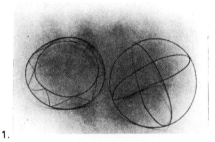

1.

3

2.

CENTRE-PIECE WITH CANDLES

1.

2.

3.

1. The finished decoration is shown in conjunction with an 'Oasis' container. Note that a block of 'Oasis' is used as a large number of stems are involved in the arrangement.

Spraying and Glittering

2. When painting foliages or dried material for use in arrangements it is much easier and quicker to use Aerosol paints. If, however, large quantities are required a paint sprayer will be cheaper and faster.

3. Glitter in the form of tiny flakes is available in gold, silver, red, blue, green and white (artificial snow or frost). It is sold by weight and it is applied by sprinkling on a painted surface before paint is dry.

If it is required to glitter unpainted material, smears of liquid adhesive are first applied where necessary to accept the glitter.

This attractive table centre-piece incorporates in its assembly silvered eucalyptus populus, laurel leaves, grevillea, dried poppy heads, white cowrushes, fir cones, baubles, ribbon and 'Flowerlite' candles. Note how the careful choice of ribbon colour adds to the cold, frosty, winter-like effect.

WALL PLAQUE

1.

2.

3.

Covering the Plaque

1. A circular plaque, either a cakeboard or specially cut from hardboard, is about to be covered with kitchen foil or textile material.

2. The foil is wrapped around the circular board and trimmed at the back as shown, and 'Sellotaped' to the plaque. An adhesive is better than 'Sellotape' when textile materials are used for covering.

3. A block of 'Oasis' has also been wrapped in foil and stuck with strong glue to the board. The 'Oasis' must be wrapped as it will not accept adhesives on its own.

A handle should be fixed to the back of the covered baseboard before commencing the arrangement.

This versatile type of decoration can be used as a Christmas doorknocker or hung on the wall. The base board has been covered with red velvet and the following ingredients incorporated:— red grasses, gilded honesty, skeleton magnolia leaves, miniature fir cones, baubles and ribbon loops.

Note how the central red ball bauble has been surrounded by magnolia leaves to give a flower-like effect.

CHRISTMAS FLOWER ARRANGEMENT

An attractive arrangement of fresh flowers and seasonal foliage consisting of red carnations, variegated holly, eucalyptus populus and blue pine.

Assembly of a Triangular Arrangement

1. The first stage with any arrangement is to establish the outline—unless you start right there will be difficulty in producing a competent arrangement. Here is shown the incorporation of first nine flowers which provide the three points of the triangle.

2. Seven more flowers have been inserted to finish off the sides of the triangle.

3. The remaining three flowers fill in the centre and when fill-in foliage has been added the arrangement is complete.

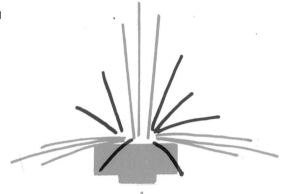

2.

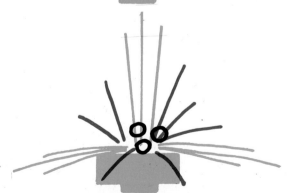

1.

3.

RED AND GOLD TABLE CENTRE-PIECE

This arrangement is in an inexpensive 'Oasis' container and consists of red grasses, gilded poppy heads, gilded fir cones, gilded old man's beard, skeleton magnolia leaves, baubles, red bullrushes and ribbon loops.

Assembly of an All-the-way-round Arrangement

1. The first four flowers give the overall length of the arrangement.
2. The three bullrushes establish the height.
3. Five more ingredients are added to the visible side of the arrangement. Three of these (the lowest ones) together with their counterparts in the other side of the arrangement establish the width. The other two ingredients show the start of the building-up process.

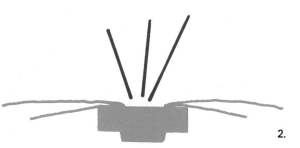

2.

1

3

CHRISTMAS CRACKER

This amusing seasonal novelty would be particularly suitable for a children's party. Being inexpensive to produce and also quick to assemble the Cracker will commend itself to those whose time is strictly limited.

The contents of the decorative spray are silvered twigs, silvered poppy heads, one wood rose, silvered fern, red grasses, ribbon and mini baubles.

Dried Material

Whilst it may not be considered really necessary for the shops to stock up and sell Christmas cards as early as September it is however very desirable to start collecting suitable dried material for Christmas arrangements from the late Summer onwards.

A hoard of fir cones, bracken, seed heads etc can come in extremely useful to provide interesting variety to the decoration and the collection can be increased in its scope by selecting from the vast range of dried material which is now constantly coming from all over the world. Some of the tropical seed heads, preserved flowers and foliages provide unusual shapes to contrast with the more orthodox locally collected items.

Driftwood, from the tide line, collected whilst at the seaside, with its weird and grotesque shapes, can be the making of a decoration. In the same category come bare branches of unusual shapes. So no visit to the sea or countryside should prove fruitless in this respect.

Cork bark, mainly from North Africa and Spain, is also a useful accessory. It is light in weight and can be bought from most flower shops and sundriesmen.

Construction of Cracker

Four cylinders of 'Oasis' are next to the finished cracker. These cylinders are rolled in red foil and provide a base not only to preserve the cylinder shape but also to accept the floral spray ingredients. A hole is cut in the foil for the latter purpose. Note how the two ends of the Cracker are tied. 'Sellotape' can also be used for this purpose.

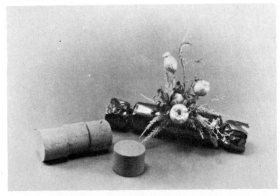

GOLD AND ORANGE ARRANGEMENT

A.

2.

1

3.

It would be usual to see the counterpart of this arrangement used in conjunction, on either side of a sideboard or mantelpiece.

The arrangement includes teazles, bullrushes, ribbon roses (see pages 6 and 7), gilded laurel leaves and foliages.

Assembly of an 'L'-shaped arrangement

(A). This shows the final arrangement next to the boat-shaped candlestick holder container. Note the block of 'Oasis' to accept the ingredients.

1. The first five items establish the vertical and the horizontal of the 'L'.

2. The three ribbon roses are positioned to provide a focal point.

3. Leaves are tucked around the roses leaving small gaps still to be filled. Note that in this case the very powerful focal point has been established at an earlier stage than perhaps would be the case normally.

PLANTED BOWL

This colourful bowl of plants will last well and will represent very good value. The plants used are poinsettia, kalanchöe, euonymus variegata, peperomia Magnoliaefolia and pilea together with ribbon clusters. (See page 36.)

Before planting the bowl it is advisable to arrange the plants so that their final position is borne in mind, with the taller subjects at the back. A peaty compost should be used so that moisture will be retained. Be careful to restrict the compost level to $\frac{1}{2}$ in. below the rim of the bowl to allow for watering.

At Christmastide there are a large selection of flowering plants available and a list of some of these is given below :—

Azalea Indica. These colourful plants are mainly grown in Belgium and forced into flower after being imported. They need watering every day as the pot in which they are planted is almost completely filled with roots. Total immersion in a basin or bucket until the bubbles stop is the most reliable method.

Chrysanthemums. These are now grown on an all-the-year-round basis by specialist growers. Special lighting, shading, dwarfing and environmental techniques are employed to produce this colourful, long-lasting subject.

Cineraria. A very gay and colourful daisy-flowered plant. Tend to be rather heavily forced to flower at Christmas so not always completely reliable. Be careful when watering—too much or too little can be disastrous.

Cyclamen. A beautiful, long-lasting plant. The silver-leaved varieties are particularly attractive and less susceptible to botrytis. Don't totally immerse when watering and keep the corm free of water otherwise it will rot.

Hyacinths. Have every property one could hope to find with a flowering plant. They have a good colour range, a beautiful scent and are long-suffering when only given the minimum of attention.

Kalanchöe. Are a popular smallish plant available in red or pale yellow. Considerable skill is required to bring them into flower for Christmas.

Poinsettia. This is a comparatively new Christmas plant made possible by extensive research into dwarfing agents so as to ensure a bushy, shapely plant. Primarily available in red, pink and cream are also available from time to time.

Solanum. New varieties of this 'Winter Cherry' plant now ensure a mass of beautiful red/orange berries and, with care, these together with the foliage can be kept going for many months.

For details of planting bowls see *AUTUMN FLOWER ARRANGING* by the same Author.

TABLE ARRANGEMENT WITH CANDLE

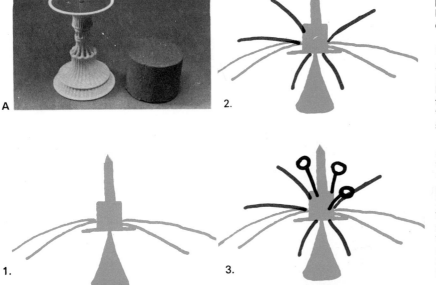

A delicate decoration for the dining table, containing gilded eucalyptus populus and skeleton magnolia leaves, big and mini baubles and ribbon. A cream candle to tone with ingredients.

Container for Candle Arrangement

(A). This container requires a cylindrical block of 'Oasis' which is positioned onto the spike. As there are no sides the 'Oasis' should be wrapped in foil, after soaking, to avoid drips on the table.

Assembly of an All-the-way-round Arrangement

1. The first four items go to create the length of the arrangement.
2. The two items projecting over the front (together with their opposite numbers behind—not visible) establish the width. A further three ingredients commence the building-up process.
3. The three gold baubles give a point of interest. Note the variation in height.

ROBIN REDBREAST ARRANGEMENT

This charming natural Christmas arrangement incorporates the following items :—bullrushes, teazles, natural grasses, wood roses, skeleton magnolia leaves, preserved beech and other foliages, a shapely twig and two birds.

The cork bark has been selected for the approximate length required and used in conjunction with 'Polyfilla' as the base. An aerosol containing artificial snow has been used to lightly dust the whole decoration. The preservation of leaves, foliages, seed heads, flowers, etc are dealt with in some detail in the companion volume called 'Dried Flower Arranging'. For those, who lack the time or facility to carry out the work themselves, there are extensive ranges of preserved material stocked by most flower shops.

1.

1. This shows the back of the arrangement with the mound of 'Polyfilla' (invisible from the front) securing all the ingredients. The use of a 'Polyfilla' base precludes the incorporation of any fresh flowers owing to the lack of moisture.

2. A close-up of the robin showing how it is fixed with wire by the feet to the branch.

The other robin is fixed to the cork bark with a small amount of 'Polyfilla'.

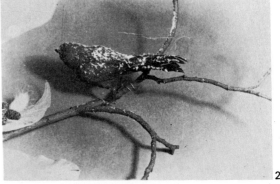

2.

ORANGE TREE

1.

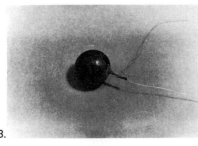

3.

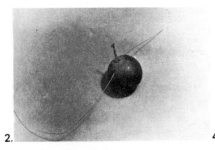

2.

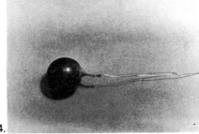

4.

This unusual Christmas notion is versatile as far as locations are concerned. The ingredients used are various foliages, lichen or reindeer moss and individual berries from a solanum plant.

Material required for Orange Tree

1. The complete orange tree is shown with the following items which are required for its construction. A container filled with 'Oasis', bun moss for finally covering the 'Oasis'. An 'Oasis' ball with its ribbon-covered stick.

Wiring a Single Solanum Berry

2. A thin silver rose wire is passed through the berry and out the other side.
3. After the wire has been bent into a hairpin shape, one leg is wound around the small berry stem and the other leg.
4. The berry now wired and ready for use.

BLUE AND SILVER TABLE CENTRE

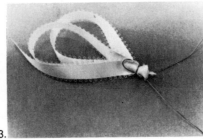

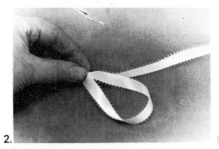

Container for Table Centre

1. This is the container which has been used for the table centre decoration. Any bowl could be used but where elegant table appointments are being used a container of quality is desirable.

Making a Ribbon Cluster

2. A loop of ribbon is held with finger and thumb whilst another loop is made and retained in a similar fashion.

3. When the required number of loops has been assembled a wire (10 in. by 22°) is hairpinned and one leg is wound around the other leg and the base of the ribbon loops. The two legs are then paralleled and the cluster is ready for insertion.

A pretty centre-piece with seasonal connotations consisting of silvered old man's beard, poppy heads, fir cones (see page 5 for wiring details), skeleton magnolia leaves, silvered fern, ball baubles, ribbon clusters and candles.

The arrangement should be kept fairly low in relation to the candles as these cannot be allowed to burn down too far without danger of the dried ingredients igniting.

HOLLY DOORKNOCKER

The American custom of celebrating Christmas-tide by hanging a welcoming seasonal decoration on the front door is rapidly becoming accepted in the United Kingdom. This decoration is simple but effective and red ribbons and baubles have been used to provide the colour with a background of sombre evergreens. Instead of using only holly and blue pine as the base, berries, mistletoe and/or fir cones could well be incorporated.

Christmas Flowers and Foliages
With ever-increasing air transport, the seasons now have little effect upon flower availability. Nevertheless there are certain flowers and foliage which are more appropriate at Christmas-time and information is given below.

Anemones. From France and Devon and Cornwall.

Carnations. Red and white, particularly good from overseas where light intensity is better.

Chrysanthemums. Particularly white blooms.

Gladioli. White and red from South Africa and Kenya.

Hellebore. Christmas Roses in white, expensive and mainly from Holland.

Ranunculus. Double red from the south of France.

Tulips. Red. The first forced ones from Lincolnshire.

Foliages. Blue pine is one of the best and does not drop its needles. Camellia is expensive but lasts very well. Laurel, Portuguese laurel and yew are all cheap. Eucalyptus populus and grevillea are both attractive foliages from the Côte d'Azur.

Making a Doorknocker
The photograph shows the completed Doorknocker with a polystyrene frame next to it. The frame is used as a base and the various ingredients are wired and inserted into position. Details of wiring are given in other parts of the book. Instead of the polystyrene ring it would be possible to use a wire coat-hanger. This should be bent into the shape of a circle and the ingredients bound on with reel wire.

RED AND GOLD CENTRE-PIECE *(Cover Picture)*

A festive table arrangement equally suitable for a desk or coffee table.

Arranged in a candle holder container, the decoration contains gilded foliages, gold miniature fir cones, red grasses, various baubles, ribbon clusters and candle.

OTHER TITLES AVAILABLE

SERIES I
Spring Flower Arranging
Summer Flower Arranging
Autumn Flower Arranging
Winter Flower Arranging

These books show in detail the elaborate assembly techniques required to produce arrangements with a professional polish. Also many valuable hints and tips on flowers and flower decoration are given.

SERIES 2
Party Flower Arranging
Church Flower Arranging
Dried Flower Arranging

These books are the companion volumes with Christmas Flower Arranging and are full of interesting information as well as a large number of sophisticated flower decorations.

FLORISTRY SERIES
The Art of Floristry—Wedding Flowers
The Art of Floristry—Funeral Flowers

These two books are each illustrated with over 400 step-by-step photographs showing the intricate techniques required to make up all types of wedding bouquets, headdresses etc, as well as funeral tributes.

Wedding Flowers in Colour
Gift and Sympathy Flowers in Colour

Two design books showing a comprehensive range of Wedding Flowers, Funeral Tributes and Gift Flowers—all in full colour.

An important educational development

ELF. A new colourful fun course which enables parents to teach their young children the 3R's at home.